The Poetry of Bliss Carman

Volume III -Behind the Arras

A Book of the Unseen

William Bliss Carman was born in Fredericton, in New Brunswick on April 15th 1861. He was educated at Fredericton Collegiate School before moving to the University of New Brunswick, obtaining his B.A. there in 1881. As is common with so many writers his first published piece was for the University magazine and for Carman that was in 1879.

After several years editing various magazines and periodicals Carman first published a poetry volume in 1893 with Low Tide on Grand Pré. There was no Canadian company prepared to publish and when an American company did so it went bankrupt.

The following year was decidedly better. His partnership with the American poet Richard Hovey had given birth to Songs of Vagabondia. It was an immediate success.

That success prompted the Boston firm, Stone & Kimball, to reissue Low Tide on Grand Pré and to hire Carman as the editor of its literary journal, The Chapbook.

Carman brought out, in 1895, Behind the Arras, a somewhat more serious and philosophical work centered on the premise of a long meditation, using the speaker's house and its many rooms, as a symbol of life and the choices to be made.

In 1896 Carman met Mrs Mary Perry King, who rapidly became patron, adviser and sometime lover. She also became his writing collaborator on two verse dramas.

In 1897 Carman published Ballad of Lost Haven, and in 1898, By the Aurelian Wall, the title poem itself was an elegy to John Keats and the book was a collection of formal elegies.

As the century turned Carman was hard at work on a five-volume set of poetry "Pans Pipes". The excellence of a number of these poems did much to install Carman as the most noted of Canadian Poets and eventually their own Poet Laureate.

In 1912 the final work in the Vagabondia series was published. Richard Hovey had died in 1900 and so this last work was purely Carman's. It has a distinct elegiac tone as if remembering the past works themselves.

On October 28th, 1921 Carman was honored by the newly-formed Canadian Authors' Association where he was crowned Canada's Poet Laureate with a wreath of maple leaves.

William Bliss Carman died of a brain hemorrhage at the age of 68 in New Canaan on the 8th June, 1929.

Index of Contents

To G. H. B.

"I shut myself in with my soul,
And the shapes come eddying forth."

Behind the Arras

I like the old house tolerably well,
Where I must dwell
Like a familiar gnome;
And yet I never shall feel quite at home:
I love to roam.

Day after day I loiter and explore
From door to door;
So many treasures lure
The curious mind. What histories obscure
They must immure!

I hardly know which room I care for best;

This fronting west,
With the strange hills in view,
Where the great sun goes,—where I may go too,
When my lease is through,—

Or this one for the morning and the east,
Where a man may feast
His eyes on looming sails,
And be the first to catch their foreign hails
Or spy their bales.

Then the pale summer twilights towards the pole!
It thrills my soul
With wonder and delight,
When gold-green shadows walk the world at night,
So still, so bright.

There at the window many a time of year,
Strange faces peer,
Solemn though not unkind,
Their wits in search of something left behind
Time out of mind;

As if they once had lived here, and stole back
To the window crack
For a peep which seems to say,
"Good fortune, brother, in your house of clay!"
And then, "Good day!"

I hear their footsteps on the gravel walk,
Their scraps of talk,
And hurrying after, reach
Only the crazy sea-drone of the beach
In endless speech.

And often when the autumn noons are still,
By swale and hill
I see their gipsy signs,
Trespassing somewhere on my border lines;
With what designs?

I forth afoot; but when I reach the place,
Hardly a trace,
Save the soft purple haze
Of smouldering camp-fires, any hint betrays
Who went these ways.

Or tatters of pale aster blue, descried

By the roadside,
Reveal whither they fled;
Or the swamp maples, here and there a shred
Of Indian red.

But most of all, the marvellous tapestry
Engrosses me,
Where such strange things are rife,
Fancies of beasts and flowers, and love and strife,
Woven to the life;

Degraded shapes and splendid seraph forms,
And teeming swarms
Of creatures gauzy dim
That cloud the dusk, and painted fish that swim,
At the weaver's whim;

And wonderful birds that wheel and hang in the air;
And beings with hair,
And moving eyes in the face,
And white bone teeth and hideous grins, who race
From place to place;

They build great temples to their John-a-nod,
And fume and plod
To deck themselves with gold,
And paint themselves like chattels to be sold,
Then turn to mould.

Sometimes they seem almost as real as I;
I hear them sigh;
I see them bow with grief,
Or dance for joy like an aspen leaf;
But that is brief.

They have mad wars and phantom marriages;
Nor seem to guess
There are dimensions still,
Beyond thought's reach, though not beyond love's will,
For soul to fill.

And some I call my friends, and make believe
Their spirits grieve,
Brood, and rejoice with mine;
I talk to them in phrases quaint and fine
Over the wine;

I tell them all my secrets; touch their hands;

One understands
Perhaps. How hard he tries
To speak! And yet those glorious mild eyes,
His best replies!

I even have my cronies, one or two,
My cherished few.
But ah, they do not stay!
For the sun fades them and they pass away,
As I grow gray.

Yet while they last how actual they seem!
Their faces beam;
I give them all their names,
Bertram and Gilbert, Louis, Frank and James,
Each with his aims;

One thinks he is a poet, and writes verse
His friends rehearse;
Another is full of law;
A third sees pictures which his hand can draw
Without a flaw.

Strangest of all, they never rest. Day long
They shift and throng,
Moved by invisible will,
Like a great breath which puffs across my sill,
And then is still;

It shakes my lovely manikins on the wall;
Squall after squall,
Gust upon crowding gust,
It sweeps them willy nilly like blown dust
With glory or lust.

It is the world-ghost, the time-spirit, come
None knows where from,
The viewless draughty tide
And wash of being. I hear it yaw and glide,
And then subside,

Along these ghostly corridors and halls
Like faint footfalls;
The hangings stir in the air;
And when I start and challenge, "Who goes there?"
It answers, "Where?"

The wail and sob and moan of the sea's dirge,

Its plangor and surge;
The awful biting sough
Of drifted snows along some arctic bluff,
That veer and luff,

And have the vacant boding human cry,
As they go by;—
Is it a banished soul
Dredging the dark like a distracted mole
Under a knoll?

Like some invisible henchman old and gray,
Day after day
I hear it come and go,
With stealthy swift unmeaning to and fro,
Muttering low,

Ceaseless and daft and terrible and blind,
Like a lost mind.
I often chill with fear
When I bethink me, What if it should peer
At my shoulder here!

Perchance he drives the merry-go-round whose track
Is the zodiac;
His name is No-man's-friend;
And his gabbling parrot-talk has neither trend,
Beginning, nor end.

A prince of madness too, I'd cry, "A rat!"
And lunge thereat,—
Let out at one swift thrust
The cunning arch-delusion of the dust
I so mistrust,

But that I fear I should disclose a face
Wearing the trace
Of my own human guise,
Piteous, unharmful, loving, sad, and wise,
With the speaking eyes.

I would the house were rid of his grim pranks,
Moaning from banks
Of pine trees in the moon,
Startling the silence like a demoniac loon
At dead of noon,

Or whispering his fool-talk to the leaves

About my eaves.
And yet how can I know
'T is not a happy Ariel masking so
In mocking woe?

Then with a little broken laugh I say,
Snatching away
The curtain where he grinned
(My feverish sight thought) like a sin unsinned,
"Only the wind!"

Yet often too he steals so softly by,
With half a sigh,
I deem he must be mild,
Fair as a woman, gentle as a child,
And forest wild.

Passing the door where an old wind-harp swings,
With its five strings,
Contrived long years ago
By my first predecessor bent to show
His handcraft so,

He lays his fingers on the æolian wire,
As a core of fire
Is laid upon the blast
To kindle and glow and fill the purple vast
Of dark at last.

Weird wise and low, piercing and keen and glad,
Or dim and sad
As a forgotten strain
Born when the broken legions of the rain
Swept through the plain—

He plays, like some dread veiled mysteriarch,
Lighting the dark,
Bidding the spring grow warm,
The gendering merge and loosing of spirit in form,
Peace out of storm.

For music is the sacrament of love;
He broods above
The virgin silence, till
She yields for rapture shuddering, yearning still
To his sweet will.

I hear him sing, "Your harp is like a mesh,

Woven of flesh
And spread within the shoal
Of life, where runs the tide-race of the soul
In my control.

"Though my wild way may ruin what it bends,
It makes amends
To the frail downy clocks,
Telling their seed a secret that unlocks
The granite rocks.

"The womb of silence to the crave sound
Is heaven unfound,
Till I, to soothe and slake
Being's most utter and imperious ache,
Bid rhythm awake.

"If with such agonies of bliss, my kin,
I enter in
Your prison house of sense,
With what a joyous freed intelligence
I shall go hence."

I need no more to guess the weaver's name,
Nor ask his aim,
Who hung each hall and room
With swarthy-tinged vermilion upon gloom;
I know that loom.

Give me a little space and time enough,
From ravelings rough
I could revive, reweave,
A fabric of beauty art might well believe
Were past retrieve.

O men and women in that rich design,
Sleep-soft, sun-fine,
Dew-tenuous and free,
A tone of the infinite wind-themes of the sea,
Borne in to me,

Reveals how you were woven to the might
Of shadow and light.
You are the dream of One
Who loves to haunt and yet appears to shun
My door in the sun;

As the white roving sea tern fleck and skim

The morning's rim;
Or the dark thrushes clear
Their flutes of music leisurely and sheer,
Then hush to hear.

I know him when the last red brands of day
Smoulder away,
And when the vernal showers
Bring back the heart to all my valley flowers
In the soft hours.

O hand of mine and brain of mine, be yours,
While time endures,
To acquiesce and learn!
For what we best may dare and drudge and yearn,
Let soul discern.

So, fellows, we shall reach the gusty gate,
Early or late,
And part without remorse,
A cadence dying down unto its source
In music's course;

You to the perfect rhythms of flowers and birds,
Colors and words,
The heart-beats of the earth,
To be remoulded always of one worth
From birth to birth;

I to the broken rhythm of thought and man,
The sweep and span
Of memory and hope
About the orbit where they still must grope
For wider scope,

To be through thousand springs restored, renewed,
With love imbrued,
With increments of will
Made strong, perceiving unattainment still
From each new skill.

Always the flawless beauty, always the chord
Of the Overword,
Dominant, pleading, sure,
No truth too small to save and make endure.
No good too poor!

And since no mortal can at last disdain

That sweet refrain,
But lets go strife and care,
Borne like a strain of bird notes on the air,
The wind knows where;

Some quiet April evening soft and strange,
When comes the change
No spirit can deplore,
I shall be one with all I was before,
In death once more.

Fancy's Fool

"Cornel, cornel, green and white,
Spreading on the forest floor,
Whither went my lost delight
Through the silent door?"

"Mortal, mortal, overfond,
How come you at all to know
There be any joys beyond
Blisses here and now?"

"Cornel, cornel, white and cool,
Many a mortal, I've heard tell,
Who is only Fancy's fool
Knows that secret well."

"Mortal, mortal, what would you
With that beauty once was yours?
Perishable is the dew,
And the dust endures."

"Cornel, cornel, pierce me not
With your sweet, reserved disdain!
Whisper me of things forgot
That shall be again."

"Mortal, we are kinsmen, led
By a hope beyond our reach.
Know you not the word unsaid
Is the flower of speech?"

All the snowy blossoms faded,
While the scarlet berries grew;
And all summer they evaded

Anything they knew.

"Cornel, cornel, green and red
Flooring for the forest wide,
Whither down the ways of dread
Went my starry-eyed?"

"Mortal, mortal, is there found
Any fruitage half so fair
In the dim world underground
As there grows in air?"

"Wilding cornel, you can guess
Nothing of eternal pain,
Growing there in quietness
In the sun and rain."

"Mortal, where your heart would be
Not a wanderer may go,
But he shares the dark with me
Underneath the snow."

And the scarlet berries scattered
With the coming on of fall;
Not to one of them it mattered
Anything at all.

The Moondial

Iron and granite and rust,
In a crumbling garden old,
Where the roses are paler than dust
And the lilies are green with gold,

Under the racing moon,
Inconscious of war or crime,
In a strange and ghostly noon,
It marks the oblivion of time.

The shadow steals through its arc,
Still as a frosted breath,
Fitful, gleaming, and dark
As the cold frustration of death.

But where the shadow may fall,
Whether to hurry or stay,

It matters little at all
To those who come that way.

For this is the dial of them
That have forgotten the world,
No more through the mad day-dream
Of striving and reason hurled.

Their heart as a little child
Only remembers the worth
Of beauty and love and the wild
Dark peace of the elder earth.

It registers the morrows
Of lovers and winds and streams,
And the face of a thousand sorrows
At the postern gate of dreams.

When the first low laughter smote
Through Lilith, the mother of joy,
And died and revived from the throat
Of Helen, the harpstring of Troy,

And wandering on through the years,
From the sobbing rain and the sea,
Caught sound of the world's gray tears
Or sense of the sun's gold glee,

Whenever the wild control
Burned out to a mortal kiss,
And the shuddering storm-swept soul
Climbed to its acme of bliss,

The green-gold light of the dead
Stood still in purple space,
And a record blind and dread
Was graved on the dial's face.

And once in a thousand years
Some youth who loved so well
The gods had loosed him from fears
In a vision of blameless hell,

Has gone to the dial to read
Those signs in the outland tongue,
Written beyond the need
Of the simple and the young.

For immortal life, they say,
Were his who, loving so,
Could explain the writing away
As a legend written in snow.

But always his innocent eyes
Were frozen into the stone.
From that awful first surprise
His soul must return alone.

In the morning there he lay
Dead in the sun's warm gold.
And no man knows to this day
What the dim moondial told.

The Face in the Stream

The sunburnt face in the willow shade
To the face in the water-mirror said,

"O deep mysterious face in the stream,
Art thou myself or am I thy dream?"

And the face deep down in the water's side
To the face in the upper air replied,

"I am thy dream, them poor worn face,
And this is thy heart's abiding place.

"Too much in the world, come back and be
Once more my dream-fellow with me,

"In the far-off untarnished years
Before thy furrows were washed with tears,

"Or ever thy serious creature eyes
Were aged with a mist of memories.

"Hast thou forgotten the long ago
In the garden where I used to flow,

"Among the hills, with the maple tree
And the roses blowing over me?—

"I who am now but a wraith of this river,
Forsaken of thee forever and ever,

"Who then was thine image fair, forecast
In the heart of the water rimpling past.

"Out in the wide of the summer zone
I lulled and allured thee apart and alone,

"The azure gleam and the golden croon
And the grass with the flaky roses strewn.

"There you would lie and lean above me,
The more you lingered the more to love me,

"Till I became, as the year grew old,
Thy fairest day-dream's fashion and mould,

"Deep in the water twilight there,
Smiling, elusive, wonderful, fair,

"The beautiful visage of thy clear soul
Set in eternity's limpid shoal,

"Thy spirit's countenance, the trace
Of dawning God in the human face.

"And when yellow leaves came down
Through the silent mornings one by one

"To the frosty meadow, as they fell
Thy pondering heart said, 'All is well;

"'Aye, all is best, for I stake my life
Beyond the boundaries of strife,'

"And then thy feet returned no more,—
While years went over the garden floor,

"With frost and maple, with rose and dew,
In the world thy river wandered through;—

"Came never again to revive and recall
Thy youth from its water burial.

"But now thy face is battle-dark;
The strife of the world has graven a mark

"About the lips that are no more mine,
Too sweet to forget, too strong to repine.

"With the ends of the earth for thy garden now,
What solace and what reward hast thou?"

Then he of the earth's sun-traversed side
To him of the under-world replied,

"O glad mysterious face in the stream,
My lost illusion, my summer dream,

"Thou fairer self of a fonder time,
A far imperishable clime,

"For thy dear sake I have fared alone
And fronted failure and housed with none.

"What youth was that, when the world was green,
In the lovely mythus Greek and clean,

"Was doomed with his flowery kin to bide,
A blown white star by the river side,

"And no more follow the sun, foot free,
Too long enamoured of one like thee?

"Shall God who abides in the patient flower,
The painted dust sustained by his power,

"Refuse to the wing of the dragonfly
His sanction over the open sky,—

"A frail detached and wandering thing
Torn loose from the blossomy life of spring?

"And this is man, the myriad one,
Dust's flower and time's ephemeron.

"And I who have followed the wander-list
For a glimpse of beauty, a wraith in the mist,

"Shall be spilt at last and return to peace,
As dust which the hands of the wind release.

"This is my solace and my reward,
Who have drained life's dregs from a broken shard."

Wise and grave was the water face,
A youth grown man in a little space;

While the wayworn face by the river side
Grew gentler-lipped and shadowy-eyed;

For he heard like a sea-horn summoning him
That sound from the world's end vast and dim,

Where the river went wandering out so far
Through a gate in the mountain left ajar,

The sea birds love and the land birds flee,
The large bleak voice of the burly sea.

The Cruise of the Galleon

This laboring vast, Tellurian Galleon,
Riding at anchor off the orient sun,
Had broken its cable, and stood out to space.
FRANCIS THOMPSON.

Galleon, ahoy, ahoy!
Old earth riding off the sun,
And straining at your cable as you ride
On the tide,
Battered laboring and vast,
In the blast
Of the hurricane that blows between the worlds,
Ahoy!

'Morning, shipmates! 'Drift and chartless?
Laded deep and rolling hard?
Never guessed, outworn and heartless,
There was land so close aboard?

Ice on every shroud and eyelet,
Rocking in the windy trough?
No more panic; Man's your pilot;
Turns the flood, and we are off!

At the story of disaster,
From the continents of sleep,
I am come to be your master
And put out into the deep.

What tide current struck you hither,
Beating up the storm of years?

Where are those who stood to weather
These uncharted gulfs of tears?

Did your fellows all drive under
In the maelstrom of the sun,
While you only, for a wonder,
Rode the wash you could not shun?

We'll crowd sail across the sea-line,—
Clear this harbor, reef and buoy,
Bowling down an open bee-line
For the latitudes of joy;

Till beyond the zones of sorrow,
Past griefs haven in the night,
Some large simpler world shall morrow
This pale region's northern light.

Not a fear but all the sea-room,
Wherein time is but a bay,
Yet shall sparkle for our lee-room
In the vast Altrurian day.

And the dauntless seaworn spirit
Shall awake to know there are
What dominions to inherit,
Anchored off another star!

A Song Before Sailing

"Cras ingens iterabimus aequor."

Wind of the dead men's feet,
Blow down the empty street
Of this old city by the sea
With news for me!

Blow me beyond the grime
And pestilence of time!
I am too sick at heart to war
With failure any more.

Thy chill is in my bones;
The moonlight on the stones
Is pale, and palpable, and cold;
I am as one grown old.

I call from room to room
Through the deserted gloom;
The echoes are all words I know,
Lost in some long ago.

I prowl from door to door,
And find no comrade more.
The wolfish fear that children feel
Is snuffing at my heel.

I hear the hollow sound
Of a great ship coming round,
The thunder of tackle and the tread
Of sailors overhead.

That stormy-blown hulloo
Has orders for me, too.
I see thee, hand at mouth, and hark,
My captain of the dark.

O wind of the great East,
By whom we are released
From this strange dusty port to sail
Beyond our fellows' hail,

Under the stars that keep
The entry of the deep,
Thy somber voice brings up the sea's
Forgotten melodies;

And I have no more need
Of bread, or wine, or creed,
Bound for the colonies of time
Beyond the farthest prime.

Wind of the dead men's feet,
Blow through the empty street!
The last adventurer am I,
Then, world, good-by!

In the Wings

The play is Life; and this round earth,
The narrow stage whereon
We act before an audience

Of actors dead and gone.

There is a figure in the wings
That never goes away,
And though I cannot see his face,
I shudder while I play.

His shadow looms behind me here,
Or capers at my side;
And when I mouth my lines in dread,
Those scornful lips deride.

Sometimes a hooting laugh breaks out,
And startles me alone;
While all my fellows, wondering
At my stage-fright, play on.

I fear that when my Exit comes,
I shall encounter there,
Stronger than fate, or time, or love,
And sterner than despair,

The Final Critic of the craft,
As stage tradition tells;
And yet—perhaps 'twill only be
The jester with his bells.

The Red Wolf

With the fall of the leaf comes the wolf, wolf, wolf,
The old red wolf at my door.
And my hateful yellow dwarf, with his hideous crooked laugh,
Cries "Wolf, wolf, wolf!" at my door.

With the still of the frost comes the wolf, wolf, wolf,
The gaunt red wolf at my door.
He's as tall as a Great Dane, with his grizzly russet mane;
And he haunts the silent woods at my door.

The scarlet maple leaves and the sweet ripe nuts,
May strew the forest glade at my door,
But my cringing cunning dwarf, with his slavered kacking laugh,
Cries "Wolf, wolf, wolf!" at my door.

The violets may come, the pale wind-flowers blow,
And tremble by the stream at my door;

But my dwarf will never cease, until his last release,
From his "Wolf, wolf, wolf!" at the door.

The long sweet April wind may woo the world from grief,
And tell the old tales at my door;
The rainbirds in the rain may plead their far refrain,
In the glad young year at my door;

And in the quiet sun, the silly partridge brood
In the red pine dust by my door;
Yet my squinting runty dwarf, with his lewd ungodly laugh,
Cries "Wolf, wolf, wolf!" at my door.

I'm his master (and his slave, with his "Wolf, wolf, wolf!")
As he squats in the sun at my door.
There morn and noon and night, with his cuddled low delight,
He watches for the wolf at my door.

The wind may parch his hide, or freeze him to the bone,
While the wolf walks far from the door;
Still year on year he sits, with his five unholy wits,
And watches for the wolf at the door.

But the fall of the leaf and the starting of the bud
Are the seasons he loves by the door;
Then his blood begins to rouse, this Caliban I house,
And it's "Wolf, wolf, wolf!" at the door.

In the dread lone of the night I can hear him snuff the sill;
Then it's "Wolf, wolf, wolf!" at the door;
His damned persistent bark, like a husky's in the dark,
His "Wolf, wolf, wolf!" at the door.

I have tried to rid the house of the misbegotten spawn;
But he skulks like a shadow at my door,
With the same uncanny glee as when he came to me
With his first cry of wolf at my door.

I curse him, and he leers; I kick him, and he whines;
But he never leaves the stone at my door.
Peep of day or set of sun, his croaking's never done
Of the Red Wolf of Despair at my door.

But when the night is old, and the stars begin to fade,
And silence walks the path by my door,
Then is his dearest hour, his most unbridled power,
And low comes his "Wolf!" at the door.

I turn me in my sleep between the night and day,
While dreams throng the yard at my door.
In my strong soul aware of a grewsome terror there
Soon to knock with command at my door.

Is it the hollow voice of the census-taker Time
In his old idle round from door to door?
Or only the north wind, when all the leaves are thinned,
Come at last with his moan to my door?

I cannot guess nor tell; only it comes and comes,
As from a vaster world beyond my door,
From centuries of eld, the death of freedom knelled,
A host of mortal fears at my door.

Then I wake; and joy and youth and fame and love and bliss,
And all the good that ever passed my door,
Grow dim, and faint and fade, with the whole world unmade,
To perish as the summer at my door.

The crouching heart within me quails like a shuddering thing,
As I turn on my pillow to the door;
Then in the chill white dawn, when life is half withdrawn,
Comes the dream-curdling "Wolf!" at my door.

Only my yellow dwarf; (my servitor and lord!)
I hear him lift the latch of my door;
I see his wobbling chin and his unrepentant grin,
As he lets his oafship in at the door.

He is low and humped and foul, and shambles like an ape;
And stealthily he barricades the door,
Then lays his goblin head against my lonely bed,
With a "Wolf, wolf, wolf," at the door!

I loathe him, but I feed him; I'll tell you how it was
(Hear him now with his "Wolf!" at the door!)
That I ever took him in; he is—he is my kin,
And kin to the wolf at the door!

I loathe him, yet he lives; as God lets Satan live,
I suffer him to slumber at my door,
Till that long-looked-for time, that splendid sudden prime,
When Spring shall go in scarlet by my door.

That day I will arise, put my heel upon his throat,
And squirt his yellow blood upon the door;
Then watch him dying there, like a spider in his lair,

With a "Wolf, wolf, wolf!" at my door.

The great white morning sun shall walk the earth again,
And the children return to my door,
I shall hear their merry laugh, and forget my buried dwarf,
As a tale that is told at the door.

Far from the quiet woods the gaunt red wolf shall flee,
As a cur that is stoned from the door;
And God's great peace come back along the lonely track,
To fill the golden year at my door.

The Faithless Lover

I

O Life, dear Life, in this fair house
Long since did I, it seems to me,
In some mysterious doleful way
Fall out of love with thee.

For, Life, thou art become a ghost,
A memory of days gone by,
A poor forsaken thing between
A heartache and a sigh.

And now, with shadows from the hills
Thronging the twilight, wraith on wraith,
Unlock the door and let me go
To thy dark rival Death!

II

O Heart, dear Heart, in this fair house
Why hast thou wearied and grown tired,
Between a morning and a night,
Of all thy soul desired?

Fond one, who cannot understand
Even these shadows on the floor,
Yet must be dreaming of dark loves
And joys beyond my door!

But I am beautiful past all
The timid tumult of thy mood,

And thou returning not must still
Be mine in solitude.

The Crimson House

Love built a crimson house,
I know it well,
That he might have a home
Wherein to dwell.

Poor Love that roved so far
And fared so ill,
Between the morning star
And the Hollow Hill,

Before he found the vale
Where he could bide,
With memory and oblivion
Side by side.

He took the silver dew
And the dun red clay,
And behold when he was through
How fair were they!

The braces of the sky
Were in its girth,
That it should feel no jar
Of the swinging earth;

That sun and wind might bleach
But not destroy
The house that he had builded
For his joy.

"Here will I stay," he said,
"And roam no more,
And dust when I am dead
Shall keep the door."

There trooping dreams by night
Go by, go by.
The walls are rosy white
In the sun's eye.

The windows are more clear

Than sky or sea;
He made them after God's
Transparency.

It is a dearer place
Than kirk or inn;
Such joy on joy as there
Has never been.

There may my longed-for rest
And welcome be,
When Love himself unbars
The door for me!

The Lodger

I cannot quite recall
When first he came,
So reticent and tall,
With his eyes of flame.

The neighbors used to say
(They know so much!)
He looked to them half way
Spanish or Dutch.

Outlandish certainly
He is—and queer!
He has been lodged with me
This thirty year;

All the while (it seems absurd!)
We hardly have
Exchanged a single word.
Mum as the grave!

Minds only his own affairs,
Goes out and in,
And keeps himself upstairs
With his violin.

Mum did I say? And yet
That talking smile
You never can forget,
Is all the while

Full of such sweet reproofs
The darkest day,
Like morning on the roofs
In flush of May.

Like autumn on the hills;
At four o'clock
The sun like a herdsman spills
For drove and flock

Peace with their provender,
And they are fed.
The day without a stir
Lies warm and red.

Ah, sir, the summer land
For me! That is
Like living in God's hand,
Compared to this.

His smile so quiet and deep
Reminds me of it.
I see it in my sleep,
And so I love it.

An anarchist, say some;
But tush, say I,
When a man's heart is plumb,
Can his life be awry?

Better than charity
And bigger too,
That heart. You've seen the sea?
Of course. To you

'T is common enough, no doubt.
But here in town,
With God's world all shut out,
Save the leaden frown

Of the sky, a slant of rain,
And a straggling star,
Such memories remain
The wonders they are.

Once at the Isles of Shoals,
And it was June . . .
Now hear me dote! He strolls

Across my noon,

Like the sun that day, where sleeps
My soul; his gaze
Goes glimmering down my deeps
Of yesterdays,

Searching and searching, till
Its light consumes
The reluctant shapes that fill
Those purple glooms.

Let others applaud, defame,
And the noise die down;
His voice saying your name,
Is enough renown.

Too patient pitiful,
Too fierce at wrong,
To patronize the dull,
Or praise the strong.

And yet he has a soul
Of wrath, though pent
Even when that white ghoul
Comes for his rent.

The landlord? Hush! My God!
I think the walls
Take notes to help him prod
Us up. He galls

My very soul to strife,
With his death's-head face.
He is foul too in his life,
Some hid disgrace,

Some secret thing he does,
I warrant you,
For all his cheek to us
Is shaved so blue.

He takes good care (by the shade
Of seven wives!)
That the undertaker's trade
He lives by thrives.

Nor chick nor child has he.

So servile smug,
With that cringe in his knee,—
God curse his lug!

But him, you should have seen
Him yesterday;
The landlord's smirk turned green
At his smile. The way

He served that bloodless fish,
Were like to freeze him.
But meeting elsewhere, pish!
He never sees him.

Yet such a gentleman,
So sure and slow.
The vilest harridan
Is not too low,

If there is pity's need;
And no man born,
For cruelty or greed
Escapes that scorn.

Most of all things, it seems,
He loves the town.
Watching the bright-faced streams
Go up and down,

I have surprised him often
On Tremont street,
And marked the grave face soften,
The mouth grow sweet,

In a brown study over
The men and women.
An unsuspected rover
That, for our Common.

When the first jonquils come,
And spring is sold
On the street corners, some
Of the pretty gold

Is sure to find its way
Home in his hand.
And many a winter day
At some cab-stand,

He'll watch the cabmen feed
The pigeon flocks,
Or bid some liner speed
From the icy docks.

His rooms? I much regret
You cannot see
His rooms, but they were let
With guarantee

Of his seclusion there—
Except myself.
Each morning, table, chair,
Lamp, hearth, and shelf,

I rearrange, refreshen,
Put all to rights,
Then leave him in possession.
Ah, but the nights,

The nights! Sir, if I dared
But once set eye
To keyhole, nor be scared,
From playing Paul Pry,

I doubt not I should learn
A wondrous thing
Or two; and in return
Go blind till spring.

The light under his door
Is glory enough,
It outshines any star
That I know of.

Wirrah, my lad, my lad,
'T is fearsome strange,
The hints we all have had
Passing the range

Of science, knowledge, law,
Or what you will,
Whose intangible touch of awe
Makes reason nil.

Many a night I start,
Sudden awake,

Feeling my smothered heart
Flutter and quake;

Like an aspen at dead of noon,
When not a breath
Is stirring to trouble the boon
Valley. A wraith

Or a fetch, it must be, shivers
The soul of the tree
Till every leaf of it quivers.
And so with me.

Was it the shuffle of feet
I heard go by,
With muffled drums in the street?
Was it the cry

Of a rider riding the night
Into ashes and dawn,
With news in his nostrils and fright
Where his hoof-beats had gone?

Did the pipes, at "Bonny Dundee,"
Bid regiments form?
Did a renegade's soul get free
On a wail of the storm?

Did a flock of wild geese honk
As they cleared the hill?
Or only a bittern cronk,
Then all was still?

Was it a night stampede
Of a thousand head?
I know I shook like a reed
There on my bed.

Nameless and void and wild
Was the fear before me,
Ere I bethought me and smiled
As the truth flashed o'er me.

Of course, it was only his hand
Freeing the bass
Of his old Amati, grand
In the silence' face.

Rummaging up and down,
From string to string,
Bidding the discords drown,
The harmonies spring,

Where tides and tide-winds rove
Far out from land,
On the ocean of music a-move
At the will of his hand.

Sobbing and grieving now,
Now glad as a bird,
Thou, thou, thou
Of the joys unheard,

Luminous radiant sea
Of the sounds and time,
Surely, surely by thee
Is eternal prime.

Holy and beautiful deep,
Spread down before
The imperial coming of sleep,
Endure, endure!

And sleep, be thou the ranger
Over it wan.
And dream, be thou no stranger
There with the dawn.

Then wings of the sun, go abroad
As a scarlet desire,
Unwearied, unwaning, unawed,
To quest and aspire,

Till the drench of the dusk you drink
In the poppy-field west;
Then veer and settle and sink
As a gull to her nest.

Wind,
Away, away!
And hurry your phantom kind
Through the gates of day,

Or ever the king's dark cup
With its studs and spars
Be inverted, and earth look up

To the shuddering stars.

Blaring and triumphing now,
Now quailing and lone,
Thou, thou, thou
Of the joys unknown!

Unknown and wild, wild,
Where the merrymen be,
Sink to sleep, soul of a child,
Slumber, thou sea!

All this his fiddle plays,
And many a thing
As strange, when his mood so lays
The bow to the string.

Sleepless! He never sleeps
That I can find.
I marvel how he keeps
A bit of his mind.

There is neither sight nor sound
In the world of sense,
But he has fathomed and found
In the silvery tense

Keen cords on the amber wood.
As he wrings them thence,
Death smiles at his hardihood
For recompense.

Oh fair they are, so fair!
No tongue can tell
How he sets them chiming there
Clear as a bell.

An orchard of birds in June,
The winds that stream,
The cold sea-brooks that croon,
The storms that scream,

The planets that float and swing
Like buoys on the tide,
The north-going legions in spring,
The hills that abide,

The frigate-bird clouds that range,

The vagabond moon—
That wilful lover of change—
And the workaday sun,

Dying summer and fall,
Seasons and men
And herds, he has them all
In his shadowy ken.

He calls and they come, leaving strife,
Leaving discord and death,
Out of oblivion to life,
Though its span be a breath.

There they are, all the beautiful things
I loved and lost sight of
Long since in the far-away springs,
Come back for a night of

New being as good as their old,
Aye, better in fact,
For somehow he gilds their fine gold,—
Gives the one thing they lacked,

The breath, aspiration, desire,
Core, kindle, control,
Memory and rapture and fire,—
The touch of man's soul.

How know the true master? I know
By my joys and my fears,
For my heart crumbles down like the snow
With spring rain into tears.

Now I am a precious one!
With nothing to do
But idle here in the sun
And gossip with you

Of a stranger you have not seen,
As like never will.
I would every soul had a screen,
When the wind sets ill

In the world's bleak house, like this
Strange lodger of mine.
His presence is worse to miss
Than sun's best shine.

I put no thought at all
Upon the end,
If only I may call
Such a man friend.

And a friend he is, heart light
With love for heft,
Proud as silence, whose right
Hand ignores his left.

Yes, odd! he gives his name
As Spiritus.
But that is vague as a flame
In the wind to us.

And then (but not a breath
Of this!) you see,
All his effects, my faith!
Are marked D.V.

His cape-coat has a rip,
But for all that,
(Folk smile, suggest a dip
In the dyer's vat,—

Those purple aldermen
Who roll about
In coaches, drive till ten,
And die of gout),

I think he finely shows
How learning's crumbs
At least can rival those
Of— 'st, here he comes!

Beyond the Gamut

Softly, softly, Niccolo Amati!
What can put such fancies in your head?
There, go dream of your blue-skied Cremona,
While I ponder something you have said.

Something in that last low lovely cadence
Piercing the green dusk alone and far,
Named a new room in the house of knowledge,

Waiting unfrequented, door ajar.

While you dream then, let me unmolested
Pass in childish wonder through that door,—
Breathless, touch and marvel at the beauties
Soon my wiser elders must explore.

Ah, my Niccolo, it's no great science
We shall ever conquer, you and I.
Yet, when you are nestled at my shoulder,
Others guess not half that we descry.

As all sight is but a finer hearing,
And all color but a finer sound,
Beauty, but the reach of lyric freedom,
Caught and quivering past all music's bound;

Life, that faint sigh whispered from oblivion,
Harks and wonders if we may not be
Five small wits to carry one great rhythmus,
The vast theme of God's new symphony.

As fine sand spread on a disc of silver,
At some chord which bids the motes combine,
Heeding the hidden and reverberant impulse,
Shifts and dances into curve and line,

The round earth, too, haply, like a dust-mote,
Was set whirling her assigned sure way,
Round this little orb of her ecliptic
To some harmony she must obey.

Did the Master try the taut string merely,
Give a touch, and she must throb to time?
Think you how his bow must rouse the echoes,
Quailing triumphing on, secure, sublime!

Ah, thought cannot far without the symbol!
Help me, little brother, hold the trend.
Dear good flesh, that keeps the spirit steady,
Lest it faint, grown dizzy at thought's end!

Waves of sound (Is this your thought, Amati?),
Climbing into treble thin and clear,
Past the silence, change to waves of color,
We must say, when eye takes place of ear?

Not a bird-song, but it has for fellow

Some-wood-flower, its speechless counterpart,
Form and color moulded to one cadence,
To voice something of the wild mute heart.

Thrushes, we'll suppose, have for their tune-mates
The gold languorous lilies of the glade;
And the whippoorwill, that plaintive dreamer,
Some dark purple flower that loves the shade.

The song-sparrow tells me what the clover
Nods about beneath the gorgeous blue;
While the snowballs tell me old love-stories
Thistle-birds half hinted as they flew.

April's faith, in robin at his vespers,
Breathes a prayer too in my lilac blooms.
What the cloudy asters told the hillside,
My lone rainbird in the dusk resumes.

Bobolink is voice for apple blossom,
Breezy, abundant, good for human joys;
Oriole has touched the burning secret
Poppies hide with their deliberate poise.

Tiny twin-flowers, what are they but fancies,
Subtler than a field-lark can express?
Swallows make the low contented twitter
Lying just beyond the pansies' guess.

Yellowbird, the hot noon's warbler, pierces
Sense where tiger-lilies may not pass.
Are not crickets and all field-wise creatures
Brahmins of the universal grass?

Saffron butterflies and mute ephemera,
Doubt not, have their songs too, could we hear.
Every raindrop is a sea sonorous
As the great worlds thundering sphere to sphere.

There's no silence and no dark forever,
Clangoring suns to us are placid stars;
Swift-foot lightning with his henchman thunder
Lags behind these gnomes in Leyden jars.

Peal and flash and thrill and scent and savour
Pulse through rhythm to rapture, and control,—
Who shall say how far along or finely?—
The infinite tectonics of the soul.

Low-bred peoples, Hottentots, Basutos,
Have a taste for scarlet and brass bands.
Our friend Monet, feeling red repulsive,
Sees blue shadows in pale purple lands.

Sees not only, but instructs our seeing;
Taught by him a twelvemonth, we confess
Earth once robed in crude barbaric splendor,
Has put on a softer lovelier dress.

Feast my eyes on some old Indian fabric,
Centuries of culture went to weave,
And I grow the fine fastidious artist,
No mere shop-made textile can deceive.

Red the bass and violet the treble,
Soul may pass out where all color ends.
Ends? So we say, meaning where the eyesight
With some yet unborn perception blends.

You, Amati, never saw a sunset,—
Hear tornadoes in a spider's loom;
I, at my wits' end, may still develop
Unknown senses in life's larger room.

Superhuman is not supernatural.
How shall half-way judge of journey done?
Shall this germ and protoplast of being
Rest mid-life and say his race is run?

Softly there, my Niccolo, a moment!
Shall I then discard my simpler joys?
No, for look you, every sense's impulse
Is a means the master soul employs.

Test and use of all things, lowest, highest,
Are alone of import to the soul;
Joys of earth are journey-aids to heaven,
Garb of the new sainthood sane and whole.

Earth one habitat of spirit merely,
I must use as richly as I may,—
Touch environment with every sense-tip,
Drink the well and pass my wander way.

Ah, drink deep and let the parching morrow
Quench what thirst its newer need may bring!

Slake the senses now, that soul hereafter
Go not forth a starved defrauded thing.

Not for sense sake only, but for soul sake;
That when soul must shed the leaves of sense,
Sun and sap may solace and support her,
Stored in those green hours for her defence.

Shall the grub deny himself the rose-leaf
That he may be moth before his time?
Shall the grasshopper repress his drumbeats
For small envy of the kingbird's chime?

Certain half-men, never touched by worship,
Soil the goodly feast they cannot use;
Others, maimed too, holding flesh a hindrance,
Vilify the bounty they refuse.

He's most man who loves the purple shadows,
Yet must love the flaring autumn too,—
Follow when the skrieling pipes bid forward,
Lie and gaze for hours into the blue.

He would have gone down with Alexander,
Quelling unknown lands beneath the sun;
Watched where Buddha in the Bo tree shadows
Saw this life's web woven and undone;

Freed his stifled heart in Shakespeare's people,
Sweet and elemental and serene;
Dared the unknown with Blake and Galileo;
Fronted death with Daulac's seventeen.

So shall mighty peace possess his spirit
Whom the noonday leads alone apart,
Through the wind-clear early Indian summer,
Where no yearning more shall move his heart.

Wise and foot-free, of the tranquil tenor,
He shall wayfare with the homeless tides;
Time enough, when life allures no longer,
To frequent the tavern death provides.

Life be neither hermitage nor revel;
Lent or carnival alone were vain;
Sin and sainthood—Help me, little brother,
With your largo finder-thought again!

Lift, uplift me, higher still and higher!
Climb and pause and tremble and plunge on,
Till I, toiling after you, come breathless
Where the mountain tops are touched with dawn!

Dark this valley world; and drenched with slumber
We have kept the centuries of night.
Cry, Amati, pierce the waiting stillness
Tremulous with forecast of the light!

Cry, Amati! Melt the twilight dirges
In "Te Deums" fit for marching men!
"Good," the days are chorusing, "shall triumph;"
Though the far-off morrows whisper, "When?"

What is good? I hear your soft string answer,
"I am that whereon the round world leans,
I am every man's poor guess at wisdom;
Evil is the soul's misuse of means.

"Up through me, with melody and meaning,
Well the floods of being or subside,
The first dim desire of self for selfhood,
The last smile that puts all self aside.

"Hate is discord lessening through the ages;
Anger a false note, fear a slackened string.
Key thy soul up to the wiser manhood,
Gentler lovelier joy from spring to spring!"

Here in turn I help you, little brother,
Half surmise what you have half explained.
Store it by to ripen, and repeat it
Long hereafter as a glimpse you gained,

When the nineteenth century was dying,
From a strolling hand that held you dear,—.
Appanage of time put in your keeping
For my far-off heritor to hear.

I imagine how his eye will kindle
When he fondles you as I do now,—
Bends above you wooing like a lover,
While you yield him all your heart knows how.

I shall have been dust a thousand summers,
But my dear unprofitable dreams
Shall be part of all the good that thrills you

In the oversoul's orchestral themes.

What is good? While God's unfinished opus
Multitudinous harmony obeys,
Evil is a dissonance not a discord,
Soon to be resolved to happier phrase,—

From time immemorial permitted,
Lest the too sweet melody grow tame,
And, untouched of pathos or of daring,
Hearts should never know what hearts proclaim:

The unstained unconquerable valor,
The unflinching loyalties of love.
Or if evil be at worst a blunder
No musician ever could approve,

The mere bungling of a hand that faltered,—
Mine or his who bade the planets poise,—
What a thing unthinkable for smallness
Is your frayed E string one touch destroys.

How that sea-gull out across the bay there
Rows himself at leisure up the blue!
Evil the mere eddy from his wing-sweep,
Good the morning path he must pursue.

Good, you think, and evil live together,
Both persisting on from change to change
Through interminable conservation,—
Primal powers no ruin can derange?

Deed and accident alike unending
By eternal consequence of cause?
No. For good is impetus to Godward;
Evil, but our ignorance of laws.

Say I let you, spite of all endeavor,
Mar some nocturne by a single note;
Is there immortality of discord
In your failure to preserve the rote?

When the sound shall pass my sense's confines,
Melt away to color or thin flame,
Does it still malinger in the prism,
Falsify the crucible with shame?

Hardly. For the melody and marring,

When they put the dear oblivion on,
Are become as fresh clay for the potter,
Neither good nor bad, for use anon.

Blighted rose and perfect shall commingle
In one excellence of garden mould.
Soul transfusing comeliness or blemish
Can alone lend beauty to the old.

While the streams go down among the mountains,
Gathering rills and leaving sand behind,
Till at last the ocean sea receives them,
And they lose themselves among their kind,

Man, the joy-born and the sorrow-nurtured,
(One with nothingness though all things be,—
Great lord Sirius and the moving planets
Fleet as fire-germs in the torn-up sea,—)

Linked to all his half-accomplished fellows,
Through unfrontiered provinces to range,
Man is but the morning dream of nature
Roused by some wild cadence weird and strange.

Slowly therefore, Niccolo, and softly,
With more memories than tongue can tell,
Lower me down the slope of life, and leave me
Knowing the hereafter will be well.

Close with, "Love is but the perfect knowledge,
The one thing no failure can befall;
Lovingkindness betters loving credence;
Love and only love is best of all."

Beauty, beauty, beauty, sense and seeming,
With the soul of truth she calls her lord!
Stars and men the dust upon her garment;
Hope and fear the echoes of her word.

How escape we then, the rainbow's brothers,
Endless being with each blade and sod?
Dust and shadow between whence and whither,
Part of the tranquillity of God.

The Juggler

Look how he throws them up and up,

The beautiful golden balls!
They hang aloft in the purple air,
And there never is one that falls.

He sends them hot from his steady hand,
He teaches them all their curves;
And whether the reach be little or long,
There never is one that swerves.

Some, like the tiny red one there,
He never lets go far;
And some he has sent to the roof of the tent
To swim without a jar.

So white and still they seem to hang,
You wonder if he forgot
To reckon the time of their return
And measure their golden lot.

Can it be that, hurried or tired out,
The hand of the juggler shook?
O never you fear, his eye is clear,
He knows them all like a book.

And they will home to his hand at last,
For he pulls them by a cord
Finer than silk and strong as fate,
That is just the bid of his word.

Was ever there such a sight in the world?
Like a wonderful winding skein,—
The way he tangles them up together
And ravels them out again!

He has so many moving now,
You can hardly believe your eyes;
And yet they say he can handle twice
The number when he tries.

You take your choice and give me mine,
I know the one for me,
It's that great bluish one low down
Like a ship's light out at sea.

It has not moved for a minute or more.
The marvel that it can keep
As if it had been set there to spin
For a thousand years asleep!

If I could have him at the inn
All by myself some night,—
Inquire his country, and where in the world
He came by that cunning sleight!

Where do you guess he learned the trick
To hold us gaping here,
Till our minds in the spell of his maze almost
Have forgotten the time of year?

One never could have the least idea.
Yet why be disposed to twit
A fellow who does such wonderful things
With the merest lack of wit?

Likely enough, when the show is done
And the balls all back in his hand,
He'll tell us why he is smiling so,
And we shall understand.

Hack and Hew

Hack and Hew were the sons of God
In the earlier earth than now;
One at his right hand, one at his left,
To obey as he taught them how.

And Hack was blind and Hew was dumb,
But both had the wild, wild heart;
And God's calm will was their burning will,
And the gist of their toil was art.

They made the moon and the belted stars,
They set the sun to ride;
They loosed the girdle and veil of the sea,
The wind and the purple tide.

Both flower and beast beneath their hands
To beauty and speed outgrew,—
The furious fumbling hand of Hack,
And the glorying hand of Hew.

Then, fire and clay, they fashioned a man,
And painted him rosy brown;
And God himself blew hard in his eyes:

"Let them burn till they smoulder down!"

And "There!" said Hack, and "There!" thought Hew,
"We'll rest, for our toil is done."
But "Nay," the Master Workman said,
"For your toil is just begun.

"And ye who served me of old as God
Shall serve me anew as man,
Till I compass the dream that is in my heart,
And perfect the vaster plan."

And still the craftsman over his craft,
In the vague white light of dawn,
With God's calm will for his burning will,
While the mounting day comes on.

Yearning, wind-swift, indolent, wild,
Toils with those shadowy two,—
The faltering restless hand of Hack,
And the tireless hand of Hew.

The Night Express

Out through the hills of midnight,
Hurtling and thundering on,
The night express from the outer world
Speeds for the open of dawn.

Out of the past and gloom-wrack,
Out of the dim and yore,
Freighted as train or caravan
Was never freighted before;

Built when the Sphinx's query
Was new on the lips of peace;
Hurled through the aching and hollow years
Till time shall have release;

Stealing and swift as a shadow,
Sinuous, urging, and blind,
Unpent as a joy or the flight of a bird,
With oblivion behind;

Down to the morrow country
Into the unknown land!

And the Driver grips the throttle-bar;
Our lives are in his hand.

The sleeping hills awake;
A tremor, a dread, a roar;
The terror is flying, is come, is past;
The hills can sleep once more.

A moment the silence throbs,
The dark has a pulse of fire;
And then the wonder of time is gone,
A wraith and a desire.

Demonish, toiling, grim,
In the ruddy furnace flare,
While the Driver fingers the throttle-bar,
Who stands at his elbow there?

Can it be, this thing like a shred
Of the firmament torn away,
Is a boarded train that Death and his crew
Consorted to waylay?

His wreckers, grinning and lean,
Are lurking at every curve;
But the Driver plays with the throttle-bar;
He has the iron nerve.

We are travelling safe and warm,
With our little baggage of cares;
Why tease the peril that yet would come
Unbidden and unawares?

The lonely are lonely still;
And the friend has another friend;
Only the idle heart inquires
The distance and the end.

We pant up the climbing grade,
And coast on the tangent mile,
While the Driver toys with the throttle-bar,
And gathers the track in his smile.

The dreamer weary of dreams,
The lover by love released,
Stricken and whole, and eager and sad,
Beauty and waif and priest,

All these adventure forth,
Strangers though side by side,
With the tramp of time in the roaring wheels,
And haste in their shadowy stride.

The star that races the hills
Shows yet the night is deep;
But the Driver humors the throttle-bar;
So, you and I may sleep.

For He of the sleepless hand
Will drive till the night is done—
Will watch till morning springs from the sea,
And the rails stand gold in the sun;

Then he will slow to a stop
The tread of the driving-rod,
When the night express rolls into the dawn;
For the Driver's name is God.

The Dustman

"Dustman, dustman!"
Through the deserted square he cries,
And babies put their rosy fists
Into their eyes.

There's nothing out of No-man's-land
So drowsy since the world began,
As "Dustman, dustman,
Dustman."

He goes his village round at dusk
From door to door, from day to day;
And when the children hear his step
They stop their play.

"Dustman, dustman!"
Far up the street he is descried,
And soberly the twilight games
Are laid aside.

"Dustman, dustman!"
There, Drowsyhead, the old refrain,
"Dustman, dustman!"
It goes again.

Dustman, dustman,
Hurry by and let me sleep.
When most I wish for you to come,
You always creep.

Dustman, dustman,
And when I want to play some more,
You never then are further off
Than the next door.

"Dustman, dustman!"
He heckles down the echoing curb,
A step that neither hopes nor hates
Ever disturb.

"Dustman, dustman!"
He never varies from one pace,
And the monotony of time
Is in his face.

And some day, with more potent dust,
Brought from his home beyond the deep,
And gently scattered on our eyes,
We, too, shall sleep,—

Hearing the call we know so well
Fade softly out as it began,
"Dustman, dustman,
Dustman!"

The Sleepers

The tall carnations down the garden walks
Bowed on their stalks.

Said Jock-a-dreams to John-a-nods,
"What are the odds
That we shall wake up here within the sun,
When time is done,
And pick up all the treasures one by one
Our hands let fall in sleep?" "You have begun
To mutter in your dreams,"
Said John-a-nods to Jock-a-dreams,
And they both slept again.

The tall carnations in the sunset glow
Burned row on row.

Said John-a-nods to Jock-a-dreams,
"To me it seems
A thousand years since last you stirred and spoke,
And I awoke.
Was that the wind then trying to provoke
His brothers in their blessed sleep?" "They choke,
Who mutter in their nods,"
Said Jock-a-dreams to John-a-nods.
And they both slept again.

The tall carnations only heard a sigh
Of dusk go by.

At the Granite Gate

There paused to shut the door
A fellow called the Wind.
With mystery before,
And reticence behind,

A portal waits me too
In the glad house of spring,
One day I shall pass through
And leave you wondering.

It lies beyond the marge
Of evening or of prime,
Silent and dim and large,
The gateway of all time.

There troop by night and day
My brothers of the field;
And I shall know the way
Their woodsongs have revealed.

The dusk will hold some trace
Of all my radiant crew
Who vanished to that place,
Ephemeral as dew.

Into the twilight dun,
Blue moth and dragon-fly
Adventuring alone,—

Shall be more brave than I?

There innocents shall bloom
And the white cherry tree,
With birch and willow plume
To strew the road for me.

The wilding orioles then
Shall make the golden air
Heavy with joy again,
And the dark heart shall dare

Resume the old desire,
The exigence of spring
To be the orange fire
That tips the world's gray wing.

And the lone wood-bird—Hark,
The whippoorwill night long
Threshing the summer dark
With his dim flail of song!—

Shall be the lyric lift,
When all my senses creep,
To bear me through the rift
In the blue range of sleep.

And so I pass beyond
The solace of your hand.
But ah, so brave and fond!
Within that morrow land,

Where deed and daring fail,
But joy forevermore
Shall tremble and prevail
Against the narrow door,

Where sorrow knocks too late,
And grief is overdue,
Beyond the granite gate
There will be thoughts of you.

Exit Anima

"Hospes comesque corporis,
Quae nunc abitis in loca?"

Cease, Wind, to blow
And drive the peopled snow,
And move the haunted arras to and fro,
And moan of things I fear to know
Yet would rend from thee, Wind, before I go
On the blind pilgrimage.
Cease, Wind, to blow.

Thy brother too,
I leave no print of shoe
In all these vasty rooms I rummage through,
No word at threshold, and no clue
Of whence I come and whither I pursue
The search of treasures lost
When time was new.

Thou janitor
Of the dim curtained door,
Stir thy old bones along the dusty floor
Of this unlighted corridor.
Open! I have been this dark way before;
Thy hollow face shall peer
In mine no more. . . . .

Sky, the dear sky!
Ah, ghostly house, good-by!
I leave thee as the gauzy dragon-fly
Leaves the green pool to try
His vast ambition on the vaster sky,—
Such valor against death
Is deity.

What, thou too here,
Thou haunting whisperer?
Spirit of beauty immanent and sheer,
Art thou that crooked servitor,
Done with disguise, from whose malignant leer
Out of the ghostly house
I fled in fear?

O Beauty, how
I do repent me now,
Of all the doubt I ever could allow
To shake me like the aspen bough;
Nor once imagine that unsullied brow
Could wear the evil mask
And still be thou!

Bone of thy bone,
Breath of thy breath alone,
I dare resume the silence of a stone,
Or explore still the vast unknown,
Like a bright sea-bird through the morning blown,
With all his heart one joy,
From zone to zone.

Scituate, June, 1895.

Bliss Carman - An Appreciation

How many Canadians—how many even among the few who seek to keep themselves informed of the best in contemporary literature, who are ever on the alert for the new voices—realise, or even suspect, that this Northern land of theirs has produced a poet of whom it may be affirmed with confidence and assurance that he is of the great succession of English poets? Yet such—strange and unbelievable though it may seem—is in very truth the case, that poet being (to give him his full name) William Bliss Carman. Canada has full right to be proud of her poets, a small body though they are; but not only does Mr. Carman stand high and clear above them all—his place (and time cannot but confirm and justify the assertion) is among those men whose poetry is the shining glory of that great English literature which is our common heritage.

If any should ask why, if what has been just said is so, there has been—as must be admitted—no general recognition of the fact in the poet's home land, I would answer that there are various and plausible, if not good, reasons for it.

First of all, the poet, as thousands more of our young men of ambition and confidence have done, went early to the United States, and until recently, except for rare and brief visits to his old home down by the sea, has never returned to Canada—though for all that, I am able to state, on his own authority, he is still a Canadian citizen. Then all his books have had their original publication in the United States, and while a few of them have subsequently carried the imprints of Canadian publishers, none of these can be said ever to have made any special effort to push their sale. Another reason for the fact above mentioned is that Mr. Carman has always scorned to advertise himself, while his work has never been the subject of the log-rolling and booming which the work of many another poet has had—to his ultimate loss. A further reason is that he follows a rule of his own in preparing his books for publication. Most poets publish a volume of their work as soon as, through their industry and perseverance, they have material enough on hand to make publication desirable in their eyes. Not so with Mr. Carman, however, his rule being not to publish until he has done sufficient work of a certain general character or key to make a volume. As a result, you cannot fully know or estimate his work by one book, or two books, or even half a dozen; you must possess or be familiar with every one of the score and more volumes which contain his output of poetry before you can realise how great and how many-sided is his genius.

It is a common remark on the part of those who respond readily to the vigorous work of Kipling, or Masefield, even our own Service, that Bliss Carman's poetry has no relation to or concern with ordinary, everyday life. One would suppose that most persons who cared for poetry at all turned to it as a relief from or counter to the burdens and vexations of the daily round; but in any event, the remark referred to seems to me to indicate either the most casual acquaintance with Mr. Carman's work, or a complete misunderstanding and misapprehension of the meaning of it. I grant that you will find little or nothing in it all to remind you of the grim realities and vexing social problems of this modern existence of ours; but to say or to suggest that these things do not exist for Mr. Carman is to say or to suggest something which is the reverse of true. The truth is, he is aware of them as only one with the sensitive organism of a poet can be; but he does not feel that he has a call or mission to remedy them, and still less to sing of them. He therefore leaves the immediate problems of the day to those who choose, or are led, to occupy themselves therewith, and turns resolutely away to dwell upon those things which for him possess infinitely greater importance.

"What are they?" one who knows Mr. Carman only as, say, a lyrist of spring or as a singer of the delights of vagabondia probably will ask in some wonder. Well, the things which concern him above all, I would answer, are first, and naturally, the beauty and wonder of this world of ours, and next the mystery of the earthly pilgrimage of the human soul out of eternity and back into it again.

The poems in the present volume—which, by the way, can boast the high honor of being the very first regular Canadian edition of his work—will be evidence ample and conclusive to every reader, I am sure, of the place which

The perennial enchanted
Lovely world and all its lore

occupy in the heart and soul of Bliss Carman, as well as of the magical power with which he is able to convey the deep and unfailing satisfaction and delight which they possess for him. They, however, represent his latest period (he has had three well-defined periods), comprising selections from three of his last published volumes: The Rough Rider, Echoes from Vagabondia, and April Airs, together with a number of new poems, and do not show, except here and there and by hints and flashes, how great is his preoccupation with the problem of man's existence—

—the hidden import
Of man's eternal plight.

This is manifest most in certain of his earlier books, for in these he turns and returns to the greatest of all the problems of man almost constantly, probing, with consummate and almost unrivalled use of the art of expression, for the secret which surely, he clearly feels, lies hidden somewhere, to be discovered if one could but pierce deeply enough. Pick up Behind the Arras, and as you turn over page after page you cannot but observe how incessantly the poet's mind—like the minds of his two great masters, Browning and Whitman—works at this problem. In "Behind the Arras," the title poem; "In the Wings," "The Crimson House," "The Lodger," "Beyond the Gamut," "The Juggler"—yes, in every poem in the book—he takes up and handles the strange thing we know as, or call, life, turning it now this way, now that, in an effort to find out its meaning and purpose. He comes but little nearer success in this than do most of the rest of men, of course; but the magical and ever-fresh beauty of his expression, the haunting melody of his lines, the variety of his images and figures and the depth and range of his thought, put his searchings and ponderings in a class by themselves.

Lengthy quotation from Mr. Carman's books is not permitted here, and I must guide myself accordingly, though with reluctance, because I believe that in a study such as this the subject should be allowed to speak for himself as much as possible. In "Behind the Arras" the poet describes the passage from life to death as

A cadence dying down unto its source
In music's course,

and goes on to speak of death as

—the broken rhythm of thought and man,
The sweep and span
Of memory and hope
About the orbit where they still must grope
For wider scope,

To be through thousand springs restored, renewed,
With love imbrued,
With increments of will
Made strong, perceiving unattainment still
From each new skill.

Now follow some verses from "Behind the Gamut," to my mind the poet's greatest single achievement;

As fine sand spread on a disc of silver,
At some chord which bids the motes combine,
Heeding the hidden and reverberant impulse,
Shifts and dances into curve and line,

The round earth, too, haply, like a dust-mote,
Was set whirling her assigned sure way,
Round this little orb of her ecliptic
To some harmony she must obey.

And what of man?

Linked to all his half-accomplished fellows,
Through unfrontiered provinces to range—
Man is but the morning dream of nature,
Roused to some wild cadence weird and strange.

Here, now, are some verses from "Pulvis et Umbra," which is to be found in Mr. Carman's first book, Low Tide on Grand Pré, and in which the poet addresses a moth which a storm has blown into his window:

For man walks the world with mourning
Down to death and leaves no trace,
With the dust upon his forehead,
And the shadow on his face.

Pillared dust and fleeing shadow
As the roadside wind goes by,
And the fourscore years that vanish
In the twinkling of an eye.

"Pillared dust and fleeing shadow." Where in all our English literature will one find the life history of man summed up more briefly and, at the same time, more beautifully, than in that wonderful line? Now follows a companion verse to those just quoted, taken from "Lord of My Heart's Elation," which stands in the forefront of From the Green Book of the Bards. It may be remarked here that while the poet recurs again and again to some favorite thought or idea, it is never in the same words. His expression is always new and fresh, showing how deep and true is his inspiration. Again it is man who is pictured:

A fleet and shadowy column
Of dust and mountain rain,
To walk the earth a moment
And be dissolved again.

But while Mr. Carman's speculations upon life's meaning and the mystery of the future cannot but appeal to the thoughtful-minded, it is as an interpreter of nature that he makes his widest appeal. Bliss Carman, I must say here, and emphatically, is no mere landscape-painter; he never, or scarcely ever, paints a picture of nature for its own sake. He goes beyond the outward aspect of things and interprets or translates for us with less keen senses as only a poet whose feeling for nature is of the deepest and profoundest, who has gone to her whole-heartedly and been taken close to her warm bosom, can do. Is this not evident from these verses from "The Great Return"—originally called "The Pagan's Prayer," and for some inscrutable reason to be found only in the limited Collected Poems, issued in two stately volumes in 1905.

When I have lifted up my heart to thee,
Thou hast ever hearkened and drawn near,
And bowed thy shining face close over me,
Till I could hear thee as the hill-flowers hear.

When I have cried to thee in lonely need,
Being but a child of thine bereft and wrung,
Then all the rivers in the hills gave heed;
And the great hill-winds in thy holy tongue—

That ancient incommunicable speech—
The April stars and autumn sunsets know—
Soothed me and calmed with solace beyond reach
Of human ken, mysterious and low.

Who can read or listen to those moving lines without feeling that Mr. Carman is in very truth a poet of nature—nay, Nature's own poet? But how could he be other when, in "The Breath of the Reed" (From the Green Book of the Bards), he makes the appeal?

Make me thy priest, O Mother,

And prophet of thy mood,
With all the forest wonder
Enraptured and imbued.

As becomes such a poet, and particularly a poet whose birth-month is April, Mr. Carman sings much of the early spring. Again and again he takes up his woodland pipe, and lo! Pan himself and all his train troop joyously before us. Yet the singer's notes for all his singing never become wearied or strident; his airs are ever new and fresh; his latest songs are no less spontaneous and winning than were his first, written how many years ago, while at the same time they have gained in beauty and melody. What heart will not stir to the vibrant music of his immortal "Spring Song," which was originally published in the first Songs from Vagabondia, and the opening verses of which follow?

Make me over, mother April,
When the sap begins to stir!
When thy flowery hand delivers
All the mountain-prisoned rivers,
And thy great heart beats and quivers
To revive the days that were,
Make me over, mother April,
When the sap begins to stir!

Take my dust and all my dreaming,
Count my heart-beats one by one,
Send them where the winters perish;
Then some golden noon recherish
And restore them in the sun,
Flower and scent and dust and dreaming,
With their heart-beats every one!

That poem is sufficient in itself to prove that Bliss Carman has full right and title to be called Spring's own lyrist, though it may be remarked here that not all his spring poems are so unfeignedly joyous. Many of them indeed, have a touch, or more than a touch, of wistfulness, for the poet knows well that sorrow lurks under all joy, deep and well hidden though it may be.

Mr. Carman sings equally finely, though perhaps not so frequently, of summer and the other seasons; but as he has other claims upon our attention, I shall forbear to labor the fact, particularly as the following collection demonstrates it sufficiently. One of those other claims is as a writer of sea poetry. Few poets, it may be said, have pictured the majesty and the mystery, the beauty and the terror of the sea, better than he. His Ballads of Lost Haven is a veritable treasure-house for those whose spirits find kinship in wide expanses of moving waters. One of the best known poems in this volume is "The Gravedigger," which opens thus:

Oh, the shambling sea is a sexton old,
And well his work is done.
With an equal grave for lord and knave,
He buries them every one.

Then hoy and rip, with a rolling hip,

He makes for the nearest shore;
And God, who sent him a thousand ship,
Will send him a thousand more;
But some he'll save for a bleaching grave,
And shoulder them in to shore—
Shoulder them in, shoulder them in,
Shoulder them in to shore.

In "The City of the Sea" (Last Songs from Vagabondia) Mr. Carman speaks of the seabells sounding

The eternal cadence of sea sorrow
For Man's lot and immemorial wrong—
The lost strains that haunt the human dwelling
With the ghost of song.

Elsewhere he speaks of

The great sea, mystic and musical.

And here from another poem is a striking picture:

... the old sea
Seems to whimper and deplore
Mourning like a childless crone
With her sorrow left alone—
The eternal human cry
To the heedless passer-by.

I have said above that Mr. Carman has had three distinct periods, and intimated that the poems in the following collection are of his third period. The first period may be said to be represented by the Low Tide and Behind the Arras volumes, while the second is displayed in the three volumes of Songs from Vagabondia, which he published in association with his friend Richard Hovey. Bliss Carman was from the first too original and individual a poet to be directly influenced by anyone else; but there can be no doubt that his friendship with Hovey helped to turn him from over-preoccupation with mysteries which, for all their greatness, are not for man to solve, to an intenser realisation of the beauty and loveliness of the world about him and of the joys of human fellowship. The result is seen in such poems as "Spring Song," quoted in part above, and his perhaps equally well-known "The Joys of the Road," which appeared in the same volume with that poem, and a few verses from which follow:

Now the joys of the road are chiefly these:
A crimson touch on the hardwood trees;

A vagrant's morning wide and blue,
In early fall, when the wind walks, too;

A shadowy highway cool and brown,
Alluring up and enticing down

From rippled waters and dappled swamp,
From purple glory to scarlet pomp;

The outward eye, the quiet will,
And the striding heart from hill to hill.

Some of the finest of arman's work is contained in his elegiac or memorial poems, in which he commemorates Keats, Shelley, William Blake, Lincoln, Stevenson, and other men for whom he has a kindred feeling, and also friends whom he has loved and lost. Listen to these moving lines from "Non Omnis Moriar," written in memory of Gleeson White, and to be found in Last Songs from Vagabondia:

There is a part of me that knows,
Beneath incertitude and fear,
I shall not perish when I pass
Beyond mortality's frontier;

But greatly having joyed and grieved,
Greatly content, shall hear the sigh
Of the strange wind across the lone
Bright lands of taciturnity.

In patience therefore I await
My friend's unchanged benign regard,—
Some April when I too shall be
Spilt water from a broken shard.

In "The White Gull," written for the centenary of the birth of Shelley in 1892, and included in By the Aurelian Wall, he thus apostrophizes that clear and shining spirit:

O captain of the rebel host,
Lead forth and far!
Thy toiling troopers of the night
Press on the unavailing fight;
The sombre field is not yet lost,
With thee for star.

Thy lips have set the hail and haste
Of clarions free
To bugle down the wintry verge
Of time forever, where the surge
Thunders and trembles on a waste
And open sea.

In "A Seamark," a threnody for Robert Louis Stevenson, which appears in the same volume, the poet hails "R.L.S." (of whose tribe he may be said to be truly one) as

The master of the roving kind,

and goes on:

O all you hearts about the world
In whom the truant gypsy blood,
Under the frost of this pale time,
Sleeps like the daring sap and flood
That dreams of April and reprieve!
You whom the haunted vision drives,
Incredulous of home and ease.
Perfection's lovers all your lives!

You whom the wander-spirit loves
To lead by some forgotten clue
Forever vanishing beyond
Horizon brinks forever new;
Our restless loved adventurer,
On secret orders come to him,
Has slipped his cable, cleared the reef,
And melted on the white sea-rim.

"Perfection's lovers all your lives." Of these, it may be said without qualification, is Bliss Carman himself.

No summary of Mr. Carman's work, however cursory, would be worthy of the name if it omitted mention of his ventures in the realm of Greek myth. From the Book of Myths is made up of work of that sort, every poem in it being full of the beauty of phrase and melody of which Mr. Carman alone has the secret. The finest poems in the book, barring the opening one, "Overlord," are "Daphne," "The Dead Faun," "Hylas," and "At Phædra's Tomb," but I can do no more here than name them, for extracts would fail to reveal their full beauty. And beauty, after all is said, is the first and last thing with Mr. Carman. As he says himself somewhere:

The joy of the hand that hews for beauty
Is the dearest solace under the sun.

And again

The eternal slaves of beauty
Are the masters of the world.

A slave—a happy, willing slave—to beauty is the poet himself, and the world can never repay him for the message of beauty which he has brought it.

Kindred to From the Book of Myths, but much more important, is Sappho: One Hundred Lyrics, one of the most successful of the numerous attempts which have been made to recapture the poems by that high priestess of song which remain to us only in fragments. Mr. Carman, as Charles G. D. Roberts points out in an introduction to the volume, has made no attempt here at translation or paraphrasing; his venture has been "the most perilous and most alluring in the whole field of poetry"—that of imaginative and, at the same time, interpretive construction. Brief quotation again would fail to convey an adequate idea of the exquisiteness of the work, and all I can do, therefore, is to urge all lovers of real poetry to possess themselves of Sappho: One Hundred Lyrics, for it is literally a storehouse of lyric beauty.

I must not fail here to speak of From the Book of Valentines, which contains some lovely things, notably "At the Great Release." This is not only one of the finest of all Mr. Carman's poems, but it is also one of the finest poems of our time. It is a love poem, and no one possessing any real feeling for poetry can read it without experiencing that strange thrill of the spirit which only the highest form of poetry can communicate. "Morning and Evening," "In an Iris Meadow," and "A letter from Lesbos" must be also mentioned. In the last named poem, Sappho is represented as writing to Gorgo, and expresses herself in these moving words:

If the high gods in that triumphant time
Have calendared no day for thee to come
Light-hearted to this doorway as of old,
Unmoved I shall behold their pomps go by—
The painted seasons in their pageantry,
The silvery progressions of the moon,
And all their infinite ardors unsubdued,
Pass with the wind replenishing the earth

Incredulous forever I must live
And, once thy lover, without joy behold,
The gradual uncounted years go by,
Sharing the bitterness of all things made.

Mention must be now made of Songs of the Sea Children, which can be described only as a collection of the sweetest and tenderest love lyrics written in our time—

—the lyric songs
The earthborn children sing,
When wild-wood laughter throngs
The shy bird-throats of spring;
When there's not a joy of the heart
But flies like a flag unfurled,
And the swelling buds bring back
The April of the world.

So perfect and complete are these lyrics that it would be almost sacrilege to quote any of them unless entire. Listen however, to these verses:

The day is lost without thee,
The night has not a star.
Thy going is an empty room
Whose door is left ajar.

Depart: it is the footfall
Of twilight on the hills.
Return: and every rood of ground

Breaks into daffodils.

There are those who will have it that Bliss Carman has been away from Canada so long that he has ceased to be, in a real sense, a Canadian. Such assume rather than know, for a very little study of his work would show them that it is shot through and through with the poet's feeling for the land of his birth. Memories of his childhood and youthful years down by the sea are still fresh in Mr. Carman's mind, and inspire him again and again in his writing. "A Remembrance," at the beginning of the present collection, may be pointed to as a striking instance of this, but proof positive is the volume, Songs from a Northern Garden, for it could have been written only by a Canadian, born and bred, one whose heart and soul thrill to the thought of Canada. I would single out from this volume for special mention as being "Canadian" in the fullest sense "In a Grand Pré Garden," "The Keeper's Silence," "At Home and Abroad," "Killoleet," and "Above the Gaspereau," but have no space to quote from them.

But Mr. Carman is not only a Canadian, he is also a Briton; and evidence of this is his Ode on the Coronation, written on the occasion of the crowning of King Edward VII in 1902. This poem—the very existence of which is hardly known among us—ought to be put in the hands of every child and youth who speaks the English tongue, for no other, I dare maintain—nothing by Kipling, or Newbolt, or any other of our so-called "Imperial singers"—expresses more truly and more movingly the deep feeling of love and reverence which the very thought of England evokes in every son of hers, even though it may never have been his to see her white cliffs rise or to tread her storied ground:

O England, little mother by the sleepless Northern tide,
Having bred so many nations to devotion, trust, and pride,
Very tenderly we turn
With welling hearts that yearn
Still to love you and defend you,—let the sons of men discern
Wherein your right and title, might and majesty, reside.

In concluding this, I greatly fear, lamentably inadequate study, I come to the collection which follows, and which, as intimated above, represents the work of Mr. Carman's latest period. I must say at once that, while I yield to no one in admiration for Low Tide and the other books of that period, or for the work of the second period, as represented by the Songs from Vagabondia volumes, I have no hesitation in declaring that I regard the poet's work of the past few years with even higher admiration. It may not possess the force and vigor of the work which preceded it; but anything seemingly missing in that respect is more than made up for me by increased beauty and clarity of expression. The mysticism—verging, or more than verging, at times on symbolism—which marked his earlier poems, and which hung, as it were, as a veil between them and the reader, has gone, and the poet's thought or theme now lies clearly before us as in a mirror. What—to take a verse from the following pages at random—could be more pellucid, more crystal clear in expression—what indeed, could come closer to that achieving of the impossible at which every real poet must aim—than this from "In Gold Lacquer".

Gold are the great trees overhead,
And gold the leaf-strewn grass,
As though a cloth of gold were spread
To let a seraph pass.
And where the pageant should go by,
Meadow and wood and stream,
The world is all of lacquered gold,

Expectant as a dream.

The poet, happily, has fully recovered from the serious illness which laid him low some two years ago, and which for a time caused his friends and admirers the gravest concern, and so we may look forward hopefully to seeing further volumes of verse come from the press to make certain his name and fame. But if, for any reason, this should not be—which the gods forfend!—Later Poems, I dare affirm, must and will be regarded as the fine flower and crowning achievement of the genius and art of Bliss Carman.

R. H. HATHAWAY.
Toronto, 1921.

Bliss Carman – A Short Biography

William Bliss Carman was born in Fredericton, in New Brunswick on April 15th 1861. 'Bliss' was his mother's maiden name. She was descended from Daniel Bliss of Concord, Massachusetts, who was the great-grandfather to Ralph Waldo Emerson.

Carman was educated at Fredericton Collegiate School. Here, under the influence of the headmaster George Robert Parkin, he gained an appreciation of classical literature and was introduced to the poetry of many of the Pre-Raphaelites especially Dante Gabriel Rossetti and Algernon Charles Swinburne.

From here he graduated to the University of New Brunswick, obtaining his B.A. there in 1881. As is common with so many writers his first published piece was for the University magazine and for Carman that was in 1879.

England now beckoned and he spent a year at Oxford and then the University of Edinburgh (1882–1883). He returned home to Canada to work on his M.A. which he obtained from the University of New Brunswick in 1884.

Tragically his father died in January, 1885, followed by his mother in February of the following year. Carman now enrolled in Harvard University for a year. There he met and was part of a literary circle that included the American poet Richard Hovey, who would become his close friend, and later collaborator, on the successful Vagabondia poetry series. Carman and Hovey were members of the "Visionists" circle along with Herbert Copeland and F. Holland Day, who would later form the Boston publishing firm Copeland & Day and, in turn, launch Vagabondia.

After Harvard Carman briefly returned to Canada, but was back in Boston by February of 1890 saying "Boston is one of the few places where my critical education and tastes could be of any use to me in earning money. New York and London are about the only other places." However, he was unable to find work in Boston but was more successful in New York becoming the literary editor of the semi-religious New York Independent. There he helped Canadian poets get published and introduced them to a wider readership than they could receive in Canada.

However, Carman and work as an editor were not destined for a long career together and he was dismissed in 1892. There followed short stays with Current Literature, Cosmopolitan, The Chap-Book, and The Atlantic Monthly. Whilst these appointments provided the basis for a career and an income he was not suited to their demands. From 1895 he would only work as a contributor to magazines and newspapers whilst he worked on his volumes of poetry.

Carman first published a book of poetry in 1893 with Low Tide on Grand Pré. He had written the title poem in the summer of 1886 and it had (whilst he was still at Harvard) been published in the spring of 1887 by Atlantic Monthly. Despite its critical acceptance there was no Canadian company prepared to publish the volume. When an American company did so it went bankrupt. Life was becoming difficult for the young poet.

The following year was decidedly better. His partnership with Richard Hovey had given birth to Songs of Vagabondia and it was published by their friends at Copeland & Day. It was an immediate success. The young men were delighted at such a reception. It quickly sold out and was re-printed a number of times. Although these re-prints were small (usually 500-1000 copies) they were frequent.

On the back of this success they would write a further three volumes, which in their turn were almost as successful. They quickly became the center of a cult following, especially among students who empathized with the poetry's anti-materialistic themes, its celebration of personal freedom, and its glorification of comradeship."

The success of Songs of Vagabondia prompted the Boston firm, Stone & Kimball, to reissue Low Tide on Grand Pré and to hire Carman as the editor of its literary journal, The Chapbook. This ceased after a year when the company relocated and Carman expressed his desire to remain in Boston.

In 1885 Carman brought out Behind the Arras, a somewhat more serious and philosophical work centered on the premise of a long meditation using the speaker's house and its many rooms as a symbol of life and the choices to be made. However, the idea and its execution did not quite meld.

Signficantly, in 1896, Carman met Mrs Mary Perry King, who rapidly became patron, adviser and sometime lover. She put money in his pocket, and food in his mouth and, when he struck bottom, often repaired his confidence as well as helping to sell the work. She also later became his writing collaborator on two verse dramas.

Mitchell Kennerley, Carman's roommate wrote that, "On the rare occasions they had intimate relations they always advised me of by leaving a bunch of violets — Mary favorite flower — on the pillow of my bed." If her husband, Dr. King, knew of this arrangement he seems not to have objected. He was a great supporter of Carman's career and seemingly his wife's complicated involvement with that.

In 1897 Carman published Ballad of Lost Haven, a collection of poetry about the sea. Its notable poems include the macabre sea shanty, The Gravedigger. The following year, 1898, came By the Aurelian Wall, the title poem itself was an elegy to John Keats and the book a collection of formal elegies.

In 1899 his publisher, Lamson, Wolffe was taken over by the Boston firm of Small, Maynard & Co., who had also acquired the rights to Low Tide on Grand Pré. The copyrights to of his books were now held by one publisher and, in lieu of earnings, Carman took what would ultimately be a disastrous financial stake in the company.

As the century turned Carman was hard at work on what would eventually be a five-volume set of poetry; "Pans Pipes". Pan, the goat-god, was traditionally associated with poetry and the coming together of the earthly and the divine. The five volumes were all published between 1902 – 1905.

The inspiration for this came from Mary who had persuaded Carman to write in both prose and poetry about the ideas of 'unitrinianism.' This drew on the theories of François-Alexandre-Nicolas-Chéri Delsarte and was defined as a strategy of mind-body-spirit harmonization aimed at undoing the physical, psychological, and spiritual damage caused by urban modernity. The definition may be rather woolly but for Carman it resulted in some very fine work across the five-volume series. This shared belief between Mary and Carman created a further bond but did isolate him from his circle of friends.

The excellence of a number of these poems did much to install Carman as the most noted of Canadian Poets and eventually their own Poet Laureate. Among the most often quoted and printed are "The Dead Faun" (from Volume I), "Lord of My Heart's Elation" (Volume II) and many of the erotic poems from Volume III.

In the middle of publication in 1903, Small, Maynard failed and with it went all the assets Carman had tied up in the company.

Carman immediately signed with another Boston publisher, L.C. Page, who would publish seven new books of Carman poetry in this hectic period up to 1905. They released a further three books based on Carman's Transcript columns, and a prose work on Unitrinianism, The Making of Personality, that he'd written with Mary King.

Carman now felt secure enough to pursue his 'dream project,' namely a deluxe edition of his collected poetry to 1903. Page acquired the distribution rights on the condition that the book be sold privately, by subscription. Unfortunately, the demand wasn't there and it failed. Carman was deeply disappointed and lost faith in Page. However, their grip on his copyrights was absolute and sadly no further collected editions were to be published during his lifetime.

By 1904 his income was restricted and the offer to be editor-in-chief of the 10-volume project, The World's Best Poetry, was eagerly accepted.

For Carman perhaps his best years as a poet were now behind him. From 1908 he lived near the Kings' New Canaan, Connecticut, estate, that he named "Sunshine", or in the summer in a cabin in the Catskills, which he called "Moonshine."

With Literary tastes now moving away from what he could provide his income further dwindled and his health started to deteriorate.

In 1912 Carman published the final work in the Vagabondia series. Richard Hovey had died in 1900 and so this last work was purely his. It has a distinct elegiac tone as if remembering the past works themselves.

Although Carman was not politically active he did campaign during the World War One, as a member of the Vigilantes, who supported the American entry into the titanic struggle on the Allied side.

By 1920, Carman was impoverished and recovering from a near-fatal attack of tuberculosis. He returned to Canada and began to undertake a series of publicly successful and somewhat lucrative reading tours, saying "there is nothing worth talking of in book sales compared with reading. Breathless attention, crowded halls, and a strange, profound enthusiasm such as I never guessed could be,' he reported to a friend. 'And good thrifty money too. Think of it! An entirely new life for me, and I am the most surprised person in Canada.'"

On October 28th, 1921 Carman was honored at a dinner held by the newly-formed Canadian Authors' Association, at the Ritz Carlton Hotel in Montreal, where he was crowned Canada's Poet Laureate with a wreath of maple leaves.

Carman is placed among the Confederation Poets, a group that included his cousin, Charles G.D. Roberts, Archibald Lampman, and Duncan Campbell Scott. Carman was perhaps the best and is credited with the widest recognition. However, whilst the others carefully supplemented their income with writing novels and works for the magazines, or even other careers, Carman only wrote poetry together with a small amount of writing on literary ideas, philosophy, and aesthetics.

He continued his reading tours, and by 1925 had finally secured a new Canadian publisher; McClelland & Stewart (Toronto), who issued a collection of selected earlier verse and would now became his main publisher. Although they benefited from Carman's increased popularity and his revered position in Canadian literature, his former publisher L.C. Page would not relinquish its copyrights to his earlier works.

In his last years, Carman was a member of the Halifax literary and social set, The Song Fishermen and in 1927 he edited The Oxford Book of American Verse.

William Bliss Carman died of a brain hemorrhage, at the age of 68, in New Canaan on the 8th June, 1929. He was cremated in New Canaan and his ashes interred at Forest Hill Cemetery, Fredericton, with a national memorial service held at the Anglican cathedral there.

It was only a quarter of a century later, on May 13th, 1954, that a scarlet maple tree was planted at his graveside, to honour his request in the 1892 poem "The Grave-Tree":

Let me have a scarlet maple
For the grave-tree at my head,
With the quiet sun behind it,
In the years when I am dead.

Bliss Carman – A Concise Bibliography

Poetry Collections
Low Tide on Grand Pre: A Book of Lyrics (1893)
Songs from Vagabondia (1894)
A Seamark: A Threnody for Robert Louis Stevenson (1895)
Behind the Arras: A Book of the Unseen (1895)
More Songs from Vagabondia (1896)

Ballads of Lost Haven: A Book of the Sea (1897)
By the Aurelian Wall: And Other Elegies (1898)
A Winter Holiday (1899)
Last Songs from Vagabondia (1901)
Ballads and Lyrics (1902)
Ode on the Coronation of King Edward (1902)
Pipes of Pan: From the Book of Myths (1902)
Pipes of Pan: From the Green Book of the Bards (1903)
Pipes of Pan: Songs of the Sea Children (1904)
Pipes of Pan: Songs from a Northern Garden (1904)
Pipes of Pan: From the Book of Valentines (1905)
Sappho: One Hundred Lyrics (1904)
Poems (1905)
The Rough Rider: And Other Poems (1909)
A Painter's Holiday, and Other Poems (1911)
Echoes from Vagabondia (1912)
April Airs: A Book of New England Lyrics (1916)
The Man of The Marne: And Other Poems (1918)
The Vengeance of Noel Brassard: A Tale of the Acadian Expulsion (1919)
Far Horizons (1925)
Later Poems (1926)
Sanctuary: Sunshine House Sonnets (1929)
Wild Garden (1929)
Bliss Carman's Poems (1931)

Drama
Bliss Carman & Mary Perry King. Daughters of Dawn: A Lyrical Pageant of a Series of Historical Scenes for Presentation with Music and Dancing (1913)
Bliss Carman & Mary Perry King. Earth Deities: And Other Rhythmic Masques (1914)

Prose Collections
The Kinship of Nature (1904)
The Poetry of Life (1905)
The Friendship of Art (1908)
The Making of Personality (1908)
Talks on Poetry and Life; Being a Series of Five Lectures Delivered Before the University of Toronto, December 1925 (Speech). transcribed by Blanche Hume. 1926.
Bliss Carman's Scrap-Book: A Table of Contents (Pierce, Lorne, editor) (1931)

Editor
The World's Best Poetry (10 volumes) (1904)
The Oxford Book of American Verse (U.S. editor) (1927)
Carman, Bliss; Pierce, Lorne, editors (1935). Our Canadian Literature: Representative Verse, English and French.